IT'S TIME TO LEARN ABOUT ARACHNIDS

It's Time to Learn about Arachnids

Walter the Educator

Silent King Books
A WhichHead Entertainment Imprint

Copyright © 2025 by Walter the Educator

All rights reserved. No part of this book may be reproduced in any manner whatsoever without written per- mission except in the case of brief quotations embodied in critical articles and reviews.

First Printing, 2024

Disclaimer

This book is a literary work; the story is not about specific persons, locations, situations, and/or circumstances unless mentioned in a historical context. Any resemblance to real persons, locations, situations, and/or circumstances is coincidental. This book is for entertainment and informational purposes only. The author and publisher offer this information without warranties expressed or implied. No matter the grounds, neither the author nor the publisher will be accountable for any losses, injuries, or other damages caused by the reader's use of this book. The use of this book acknowledges an understanding and acceptance of this disclaimer.

It's Time to Learn about Arachnids is a collectible early learning book by Walter the Educator suitable for all ages belonging to Walter the Educator's Time to Eat Book Series. Collect more books at WaltertheEducator.com

USE THE EXTRA SPACE TO TAKE NOTES AND DOCUMENT YOUR MEMORIES

ARACHNIDS

Arachnids crawl, they leap, they spin,

It's Time to Learn about

Arachnids

With eight strong legs and a tough, hard skin.

No wings to fly, no buzzing sound,

Yet watch them scurry on the ground!

Spiders, scorpions, ticks, and mites,

Some are tiny, some give frights!

But don't be scared, just take a look,

They're not as spooky as in books.

No antennae like a bug,

Just simple eyes that look and hug.

Some have eight and some have two,

Watching everything they do!

Spiders weave their webs so tight,

Catching bugs in morning light.

Some make orbs, some tunnels deep,

Where they hide and sometimes leap!

It's Time to Learn about
Arachnids

Scorpions have pincers strong,

And a stinger, sharp and long.

In the desert, hot and dry,

Under rocks, they like to lie.

Mites are tiny, hard to see,

Crawling 'round so secretly.

Some live in the dirt and ground,

Others in your home are found!

Ticks latch on and take a sip,

Of an animal's skin, they grip!

Be aware when in the grass,

Check yourself when home at last!

Arachnids molt, they shed their skin,

To grow a new one from within.

As they get both strong and tall,

It's Time to Learn about
Arachnids

They leave behind their shell so small.

Unlike insects, they don't chew,

They suck up liquid, yes, it's true!

Venom helps to break things down,

Before they slurp it all around!

Arachnids help us every day,

They eat up bugs and clear the way.

So next time that you see one creep,

It's Time to Learn about
Arachnids

Just let it crawl and let it keep!

ABOUT THE CREATOR

Walter the Educator is one of the pseudonyms for Walter Anderson. Formally educated in Chemistry, Business, and Education, he is an educator, an author, a diverse entrepreneur, and he is the son of a disabled war veteran.
"Walter the Educator" shares his time between educating and creating. He holds interests and owns several creative projects that entertain, enlighten, enhance, and educate, hoping to inspire and motivate you. Follow, find new works, and stay up to date with Walter the Educator™

at WaltertheEducator.com

www.ingramcontent.com/pod-product-compliance
Lightning Source LLC
LaVergne TN
LVHW052017060526
838201LV00059B/4066